T0048373

SCHIRMER'S LIBRARY
OF MUSICAL CLASSICS

Vol. 848

O. ŠEVČIK

Op. 8

Shifting the Position

and

Preparatory Scale-Studies

For the Violin

Edited by

PHILIPP MITTELL

G. SCHIRMER, Inc.

DISTRIBUTED BY

HAL•LEONARD®
CORPORATION

7777 W. BLUEMOUND RD. P.O. BOX 13819 MILWAUKEE, WI 53213

Copyright, 1905, by G. Schirmer, Inc.
Copyright renewal assigned, 1933, to G. Schirmer, Inc.
Printed in the U. S. A

VORBEMERKUNG

DIE Hauptschwierigkeit in diesen Übungen besteht darin, die Verbindungen der Lagen so zu bewerkstelligen, dass dieselben kaum hörbar sind. Besondere Schwierigkeiten bietet der Wechsel von den höheren nach den tieferen Lagen. Um diesen Wechsel glatt zu machen, halte man die Violine mit dem Kinne fest und versuche, beim Lagenwechsel den Daumen der linken Hand so wenig wie möglich zu benutzen. Später sollen diese Übungen sogar ohne Hilfe des Daumens geübt werden, wobei der Daumen unter dem Hals der Geige gehalten wird.

Es ist von grossem Nutzen, wenn man diese Übungen zuerst gestossen, dann in mässigem Tempo gebunden übt.

DER HERAUSGEBER

PREFATORY NOTE

THE chief difficulty in these exercises consists in shifting (changing the position) so smoothly that it is hardly perceptible. Shifting downward, from a higher to a lower position, offers peculiar difficulties. In order to effect it smoothly, hold the violin firmly with the chin, and try to use the thumb as little as possible when shifting. Later these exercises are even to be practised without using the thumb, which is then held under the neck of the instrument.

It is highly beneficial to practise these exercises *détaché* at first, and then legato in moderate tempo.

THE EDITOR

2

Lagenwechselübungen.

Bei dem Einüben dieser Beispiele wiederhole man in gemässigtem Tempo:

a) jeden einzelnen Takt,

b) jeden Takt mit dem nächstfolgenden (1-2, 2-3, 3-4 u.s.w.)

c) alle Takte, die auf derselben Saite angezeigt sind (im 1ten Beispiele Takte 1-6, 7-12, 13-18, 19-25),

d) das ganze Beispiel in folgenden Tonarten, gebunden und gestossen:

Shifting (Changing the Position).

When practising these exercises repeat in moderate tempo:

(a) Each measure separately;

(b) Each pair of successive measures together; for instance 1 with 2, 2 with 3, 3 with 4, etc.;

(c) All groups of measures marked as to be played on the same string;– in the 1st Exercise measures 1 to 6, 7 to 12, 13 to 18, 19 to 25;

(d) The entire exercise in the keys given below, both legato and *détaché*.

1.

Wechsel der Lagen: 1-2, 2-3, 3-4 u.s.w.

Changes of position: From 1st to 2d, 2d to 3d, 3d to 4th, etc.

2.

Copyright, 1905, by G. Schirmer, Inc.   Printed in the U.S.A   *Copyright renewal assigned, 1933, to G. Schirmer, Inc.*

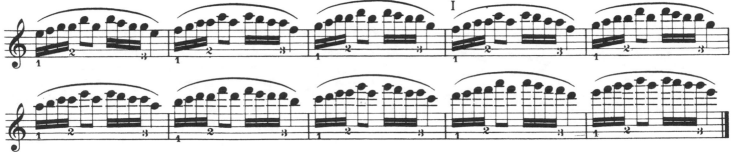

3.

4.

5.

6.

7.

Wechsel der Lagen: 1-3, 2-4, 3-5 u.s.w.

8.

**Changes of position: From 1st to 3d,
2d to 4th, 3d to 5th, etc.**

9.

10.

11.

12.

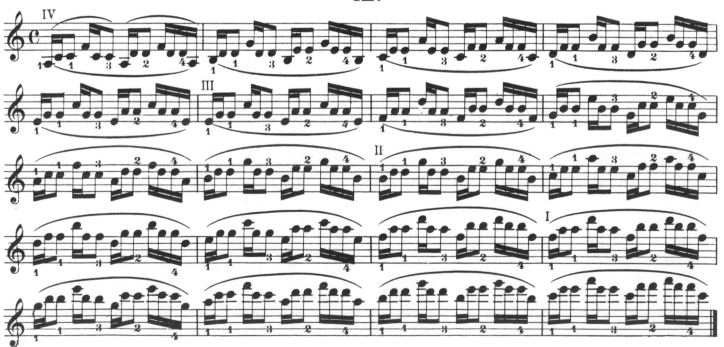

8

Wechsel der Lagen: 1-4, 2-5, 3-6 u.s.w.

16.

Changes of position: From 1st to 4th,
2d to 5th, 3d to 6th, etc.

17.

18.

19.

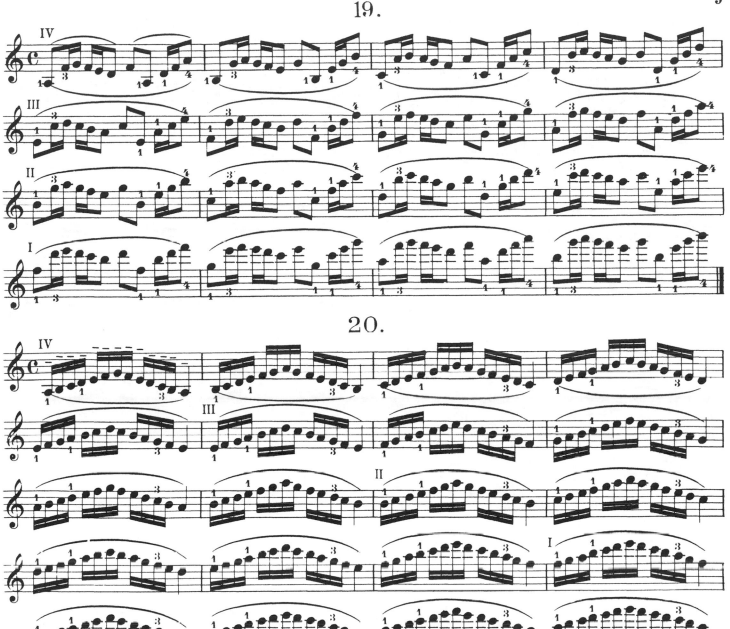

20.

21.

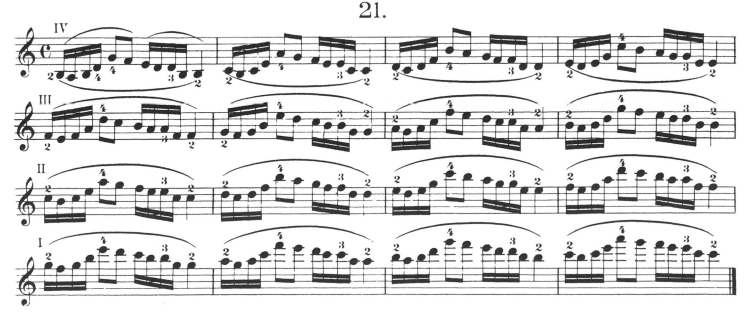

22.

23.

Wechsel der Lagen: 1-5, 2-6, 3-7 u.s.w.   Changes of position: From 1st to 5th, 2d to 6th, 3d to 7th, etc.

24.

25.

26.

27.

28.

29.

30.

31.

32.

Wechsel der Lagen: 1-6, 2-7, 3-8 u.s.w.

Changes of position: From 1st to 6th, 2d to 7th, 3d to 8th, etc.

33.

14

34.

35.

36.

37.

38.

Wechsel der Lagen: 1-7, 2-8, 3-9 u.s.w. | Changes of position: From 1st to 7th, 2d to 8th, 3d to 9th, etc.

39.

40.

41.

42.

43.

44.

45.

46.

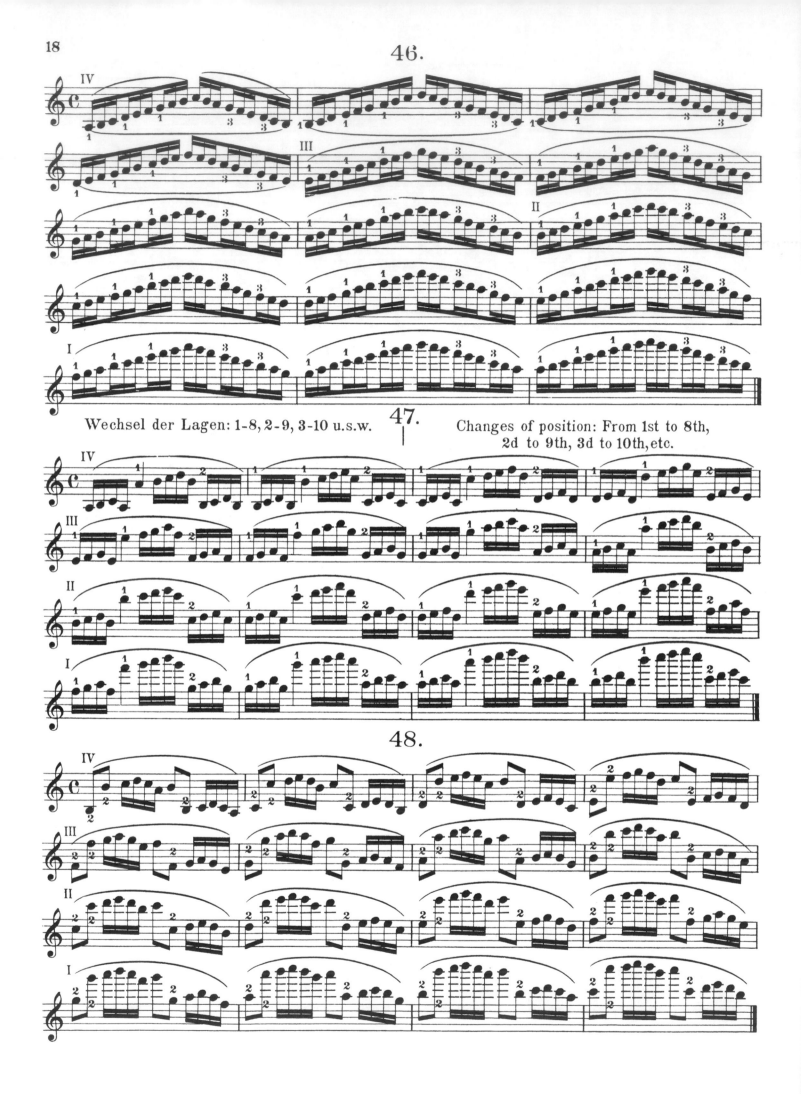

Wechsel der Lagen: 1-8, 2-9, 3-10 u.s.w.

47.

Changes of position: From 1st to 8th,
2d to 9th, 3d to 10th, etc.

48.

52.

53.

54.

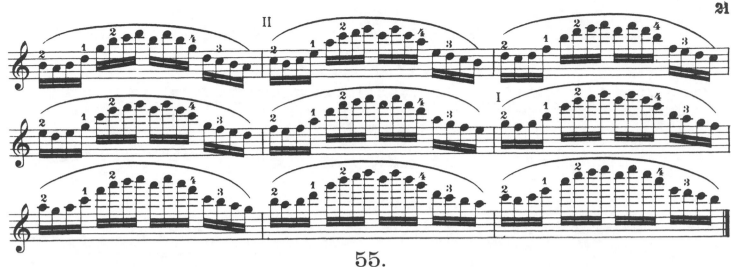

55.

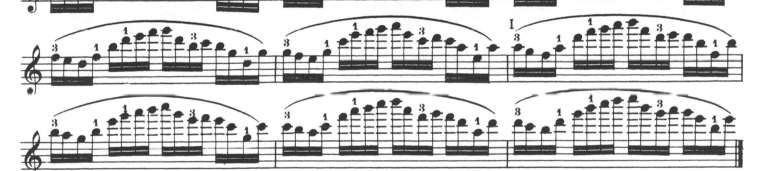

56.

57.

Tonleitern durch 3 Oktaven.　　　　Scales Throughout 3 Octaves.

C dur.
C major.

Man übe die NNº 57–59 in allen folgenden Tonarten, gebunden und gestossen:　　Practise Nºˢ 57–59 in all the following keys, both legato and *détaché*.

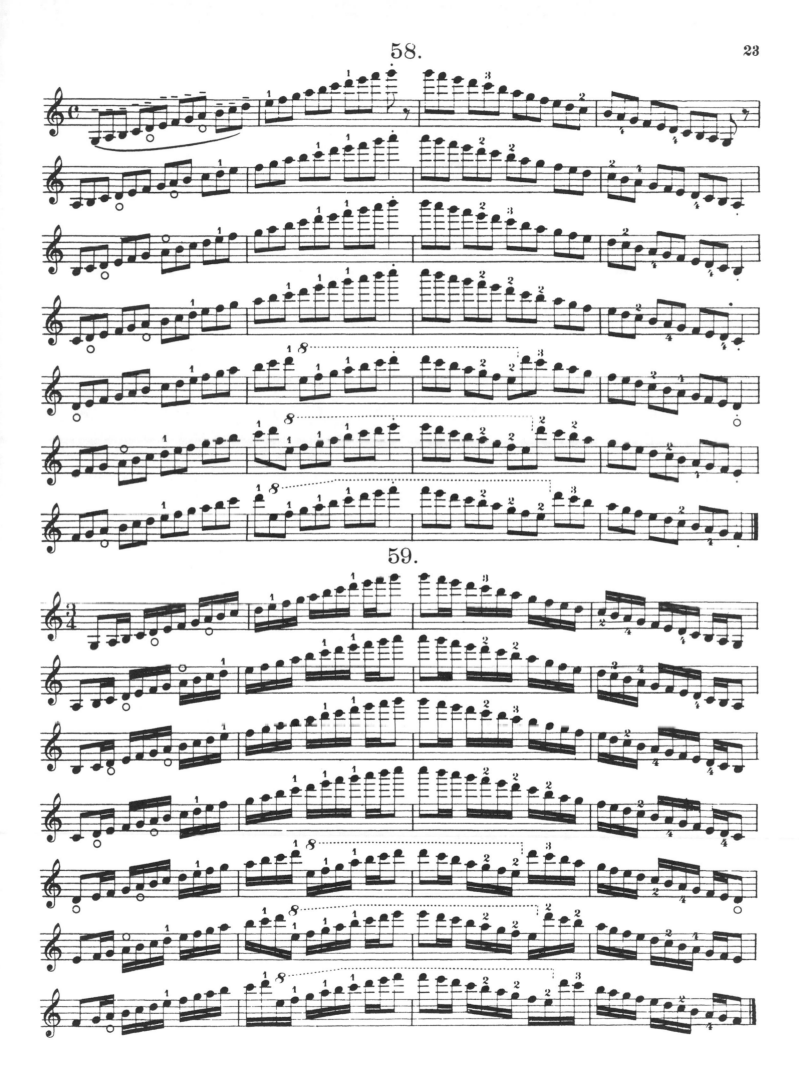